TRANSFORMING SOCIETY

A Comprehensive Introduction to Understanding Trauma, Adversity and Becoming Trauma Informed

Little Brighouse

Grosvenor House
Publishing Limited

This book is published by
Grosvenor House Publishing Ltd
Link House
140 The Broadway, Tolworth, Surrey, KT6 7HT.
www.grosvenorhousepublishing.co.uk

This book is a work of fiction. Any resemblance to
people or events, past or present, is purely coincidental.

A CIP record for this book
is available from the British Library

Paperback ISBN 978-1-80381-677-7
Hardback ISBN 978-1-80381-678-4
eBook ISBN 978-1-80381-831-3

Dedicated to the lives that
we have lost along the way,
and to the survivors whose voices
were silenced by the world.

Also to
Ade, Amanda, Kya, Pete, Tania
for their constant patience,
encouragement and guidance.

CONTENTS

Acronyms   ix

Terminology   xi

Preface   xix

Introduction   1

Background   4

Trauma and Adversity   8

   How Do We Define Trauma and Adversity?   9

   How Does Trauma and Adversity Impact
   Our Lives?   10

      In the Home   13

      In the Workplace   16

      In the Community   18

      In the Global Context   21

   What Is 'Re-traumatisation'?   24

Trauma-informed Care & Practice   27

   Trauma-informed Care   28

   Trauma-informed Practice   29

Guiding Principles of TIP & TIC   33

  Safety   34

  Trustworthiness   35

  Choice   36

  Collaboration   37

  Empowerment   38

  Culture   39

  The Four Rs   41

The Impact of Trauma-informed
Care and Practice   44

  In the Home   46

  In the Workplace   48

  In the Community   50

  In the Global Context   53

The Welsh Trauma Framework   56

Trauma-informed Organisations   60

  Cost of Becoming Trauma-informed?   60

  Trauma-informed Organisational Models   63

  Approach   65

  Key Development Areas   67

  Domains of Organisational Change   69

  Governance and Leadership   70

  Stage of Implementation   75

Taking the Next Step   77

Additional Resources   79

   Books to Discover   79

   Current Reports   80

References   82

ACRONYMS

ACE – Adverse Childhood Events

CPTSD – Complex Post-traumatic Stress Disorder

PTSD – Post-traumatic Stress Disorder

SAMHSA – Substance Abuse and Mental Health Services Administration

TIC – Trauma-Informed Care

TIP – Trauma-Informed Practice

TSW – Traumatic Stress Wales

TERMINOLOGY

ADVERSE CHILDHOOD EXPERIENCES (ACE) STUDY
A ground-breaking research study conducted by
Dr Vincent Felitti, Dr Rob Anda and colleagues that
showed the high prevalence of adversity in childhood
(ACEs), and a relationship between ACEs and
negative health outcomes through the lifespan.

ADVERSITY A difficult or unpleasant situation, set
of circumstances or experiences.

BURNOUT A gradual process of a staff members
experiencing feelings of hopelessness, fatigue
and being overwhelmed because of a lack of
support, excessive workloads and unrealistic
expectations.

CHAMPION An individual or individuals who are
trained specifically to take on roles such as
educator, trainer, mentor, coach and/or advocate
for a trauma-informed approach to ensure overall
sustainability.

CHRONIC STRESS A sustained and consistent feeling
of being pressured and overwhelmed. This occurs
over a long period of time as opposed to acute stress,

which is a physiological and psychological reaction to a specific event.

COGNITIVE APPRAISAL A thought process that interprets and evaluates new experiences, situations, potential threats and emotional responses to stimuli in the environment.

COMPASSION FATIGUE (CF) A combination of secondary traumatic stress, vicarious trauma and/or burnout that manifests in a worker.

COMPLEX POST-TRAUMATIC STRESS DISORDER (CPTSD) A condition that can arise following exposure to a major traumatic event, commonly after prolonged exposure or exposure to multiple events. In addition to the symptoms of PTSD, people with CPTSD experience difficulties controlling their emotions, feel negatively about themselves and have difficulties in relationships with other people.

DOMAINS OF CONSIDERATION Domains of organisational change that the Substance Abuse and Mental Health Services Administration (SAMHSA) cross-walked with trauma-specific content and the values and principles of trauma-informed care. These domains provide a framework for organisational change structures within each of this manual's key development areas.

GUIDING VALUES AND PRINCIPLES A framework and a lens proposed by Dr Roger Fallot and Dr Maxine Harris for individuals, organisations and systems to consider their day-to-day activities in a way that prevents re-traumatisation. Includes safety, trustworthiness, choice, collaboration and empowerment.

KEY DEVELOPMENT AREAS Ten specific aspects of organisational functioning that need to be addressed through a trauma-informed lens to best create overall trauma-informed organisational change: a key component of the trauma-informed organisational model.

PERSON-CENTRED APPROACH Where the individual is placed at the centre of the service and treated as a person first. The approach takes a co-productive, collaborative, cross-sector approach to identifying, understanding and supporting the person's needs and promotes psychological and physical safety by promoting choice, collaboration, transparency and autonomy.

POST-TRAUMATIC GROWTH (PTG) The process of making meaning out of one's experience of trauma and experiencing a positive change as a result.

RECOVERY The journey to being able to live in the present without being overwhelmed by traumatic events in the past. Recovery does not necessarily mean the complete freedom from the effects of trauma or adversity.

RESILIENCE The process of adapting to trauma and adversity; the ability to bounce back or return to the level of functioning before the trauma or adversity occurred.

RE-TRAUMATISATION When a policy, procedure, interaction or the physical environment stimulates someone's original trauma literally or symbolically triggering the emotions and thoughts associated with the original experience.

SANCTUARY MODEL An evidence-based approach for changing organisational culture to be more trauma- informed and responsive that was created by Dr Sandra Bloom and her colleagues.

SECONDARY TRAUMATIC STRESS (STS) The onset of trauma-related symptoms in a worker because of witnessing the trauma or adversity of another.

SOCIAL DETERMINANTS The broad social and economic circumstances that together influence health throughout a person's life course.

STAGES The first component of the trauma-informed organisational model that defines the things to consider, needs and resources for trauma-informed organisational change. Includes Pre-Implementation, Implementation and Sustainability.

STRENGTHS-BASED A focus on the positive attributes of a person or a group rather than the negative ones.

SYSTEMS A set of components including individuals and organisations working together as part of an interconnecting network. A system is the whole sum of the parts.

TRAUMA-INFORMED APPROACH This approach recognises that everyone has a role in facilitating opportunities and life chances for people affected by trauma and adversity. It is an approach where a person, organisation, programme or system realises the widespread impact of trauma and understands potential paths for healing and overcoming adversity and trauma as an individual or with the support of others, including communities and services.

TRAUMA Different people find different things traumatic and there are several definitions of trauma, for example SAMHSA and Blueknot. For the purposes of this document, trauma is defined as any experience that is unpleasant and causes, or has the potential to cause, someone distress and/or anxiety. It is important to note that trauma can also be used to refer to the impact of a traumatic event.

TRAUMA THERAPIES Formal, evidence-based psychological, pharmacological or other interventions that are offered within a range of settings.

TRAUMA-AWARE A universal approach that highlights that everyone from all communities have a role to play in preventing ACEs and traumatic events, providing community-led responses to the impact of ACEs and trauma, and supporting building resilience through connection, inclusion and compassion.

TRAUMA-INFORMED Taking into account that anybody could have experienced trauma and seeking to not retraumatise in our behaviours and interactions.

TRAUMA-ENHANCED An approach used by frontline workers who are providing direct or intensive support to people who are known to have experienced traumatic events within their role and encompasses ways of working to help people to cope with the impact of their trauma.

TRAUMA-SKILLED An approach embedded within the practice of everyone who provides care or support to people who may have experienced trauma.

UNIVERSAL PRECAUTION Similar to how health care professionals put on gloves to prevent the spread of blood-borne pathogens, a trauma-informed approach involves putting on metaphorical gloves (changing our interactions, policies, etc.) to prevent the possibility of re-traumatisation.

VICARIOUS POST-TRAUMATIC GROWTH (VPTG) Development of positive changes and growth in a worker's worldview because of witnessing the post-traumatic growth of others.

VICARIOUS RESILIENCE (VR) Positive meaning-making and shift of a worker's experience because of witnessing the resilience of others.

VICARIOUS TRAUMA (VT) The development of negative changes in worldview of a worker because of the cumulative impact of witnessing the trauma and adversity of others over time.

WIDER DETERMINANTS OF HEALTH The wider determinants of health are social, economic and environmental factors that influence health, well-being and inequalities.

PREFACE

Transforming Society serves as first-step introduction to trauma-informed practice and introduces the Welsh Trauma Framework as a valuable resource. It highlights the benefits and significance of transitioning to a trauma-informed organisation or service and explores the key development areas and domains of organisational change. Additionally, it introduces the concept of trauma-informed organisational models to support the implementation process.

The comprehensive introduction begins by providing a thorough yet foundational understanding of trauma and adversity, acknowledging the diverse forms, experiences and impacts. It emphasises the importance of trauma-informed practice and introduces the Welsh Trauma Framework as a valuable tool for guiding organisations in their trauma-informed approach.

Recognising the numerous advantages of becoming a trauma-informed organisation or service, *Transforming Society* highlights the positive outcomes associated with trauma-informed approaches in various contexts. These benefits include improved clinical care, enhanced prevention strategies, increased engagement with health and other services, and ultimately reduced healthcare costs. Additionally, it underscores the potential benefits for professionals and those in leadership who have experienced personal or work-related trauma.

To facilitate the transition towards a trauma-informed organisation or service, *Transforming Society* outlines the key development areas and domains that require attention. It emphasises the significance of leadership commitment, organisational assessment and the development of a trauma-informed workgroup and embedding trauma-informed approach into the organisation's ethos, vision and strategic objectives. As each industry, organisation and sector of society differs in the services they provide, a one-size-fits-all approach would unfortunately overlook and disregard the unique needs and requirements of organisation, it's staff and the clients that engage with the services provided. Therefore, *Transforming Society* is designed to be a starting-off point to inform and bring awareness to the topic and benefits of becoming trauma informed and serve as a blueprint from which to start your own trauma-informed journey. As such, adaptation and flexibility is encouraged to accommodate an organisation's specific strengths, needs and available resources, which may differ from other services and organisations.

Furthermore, *Transforming Society* introduces the concept of a trauma-informed organisational model, which outlines a structured framework for implementing trauma-informed practices. This model encompasses three stages: Preparation, Implementation and Continuation. Each stage is designed to guide organisations through specific activities and considerations of adaptation, to effectively integrate trauma-informed approaches into their operations, while avoiding the issue of creating silos or pockets of trauma-informed practise. This resource, which is currently in production, provides detailed guidance and practical tools to support organisations throughout the implementation process. Providing step-by-step instructions, resources and templates to facilitate the successful adoption of trauma-informed practices, this accompanying three-stage Implementation Guide is currently being developed and will be published following the release of *Transforming Society.*

In conclusion, this comprehensive introduction equips organisations, authorities, those in person-facing roles and individuals with the knowledge and tools necessary to acquire a foundational understanding into trauma and adversity, implement trauma-informed practices and ultimately transition to trauma-informed organisations or services. By embracing a trauma-informed approach, organisations, services and indeed we as individuals can improve effectiveness, promote well-being and create a culture of understanding and support for those they live, serve and work with. The accompanying Implementation Guide provides further support by offering practical guidance and resources to facilitate successful implementation. However, the accompanying guide is still in production and will not available before the end of 2024.

Looking towards the future, a collection of educational books on the informed care of trauma and adversity is planned with the aim of providing an advanced level of understanding and insight into trauma and adversity, its varying forms, common misconceptions and best practice, in order to support any reader on this journey of understand trauma, adversity and becoming trauma-informed.

INTRODUCTION

In the context of this document and in line with the Welsh Trauma Framework, we define trauma as any unbearable experience that causes distress or anxiety and has the potential of being an actual or perceived threat such as of death, serious injury or violence. However, all traumatic experiences can be highly distressing and significantly impact the person affected. It's important to note that the term 'trauma' can also refer to the impact of a traumatic event, and not solely to the experience itself. Changes in behaviour and emotional states may be observed in individuals who have undergone trauma or adversity, however, the presentation will vary because we as individuals all react differently to our life experiences. For example, some may not experience any distress while others may have a self-limiting response, and some may develop diagnosable conditions, including post-traumatic stress disorder (PTSD), complex post-traumatic stress disorder (CPTSD), personality disorders, anxiety disorders, substance use disorders, and though less frequently, psychosis and dissociative disorders. Furthermore, individuals from marginalised groups face additional pronounced adversity and traumatic experiences unique to their marginalisation. Some of these marginalised groups include asylum seekers and refugees, ethnic minorities, LGBTQIA+, disabled and neurodivergent people.

Structural inequality, discrimination and the social determinants of health, such as economic and social factors that influence living conditions, can directly contribute to distress and result in unequal access to support. Marginalised communities may face additional barriers to accessing support, including geographical remoteness, lack of public transport, language barriers and financial constraints.

Furthermore, limited knowledge and understanding of emotional well-being can hinder individuals from seeking help when needed or knowing what support to seek. Emotional deprivation can also prevent individuals from seeking appropriate support in a timely manner. Non-trauma-informed organisations and systems may exacerbate the impact of adversity and trauma, leading to further traumatisation. Trauma- informed organisations recognise that adversity, trauma and distress can affect anyone at any stage of life. Their aim is to create psychosocially healthy conditions for both the workforce and the individuals they support, minimising exposure to adversity, trauma and distress. They possess the confidence to understand the interventions and supportive factors required to prevent and mitigate the long-term effects on physical and mental health and well-being. Effective trauma-informed organisations allocate time and resources where they are most needed, prioritising integration, person-centredness and embodying the principles outlined in the Well-being of Future Generations Act (Wales) 2015.

This introduction to understanding trauma and adversity aims to address and provide clarity on crucial questions related to the spectrum of distress, definitions and language used in trauma-related discussions. The lack of consistency in definitions and approaches makes it challenging to evaluate the impact of adopting a trauma-informed approach. However, initial evidence suggests that trauma-informed approaches can have significantly positive outcomes for both children and adults in various services. These approaches have shown improvements in clinical care, illness prevention through identifying at-risk individuals, enhanced engagement with health and other services, leading to better outcomes and reduced healthcare costs. Additionally, trauma-informed care can benefit healthcare professionals who have a personal history of trauma or have experienced trauma related to their work.

BACKGROUND

The concept of being trauma informed and offering trauma-informed care (TIC) originated from Dr Sandra Bloom's development of the Sanctuary Model. Other experts such as Dr Roger Fallot, Dr Maxine Harris and Dr Ann Jennings have also contributed to creating a foundation for understanding and responding appropriately to the effects of trauma and adversity. The approaches to comprehensive trauma-informed treatment developed by Dr Ricky Greenwald and Dr Lisa Najavits have had a significant impact on how we address trauma. Additionally, SAMHSA's trauma-informed care in behavioural health services (TIP-57) has provided a useful tool for practical application.

In recent years, the world has become more aware of the impact of trauma and traumatic events on individuals and communities. The ongoing Covid-19 pandemic has further highlighted this issue, with many people experiencing long-term effects on their well-being due to the trauma caused by the pandemic. Trauma can lead to long-term physical and psychological effects, including increased risk of mental health disorders, substance abuse and chronic illness. Communities affected by trauma may experience decreased social cohesion, increased crime rates and economic hardship. For example, with the compounding impacts of austerity, Covid-19 and the cost-of-living crisis, those most vulnerable are likely to be victims of crime and violence.

The financial burden on public services such as healthcare, education, housing and social care is also significant. COVID-19 has exacerbated existing mental health inequalities for people in Wales, according to a new report from Cardiff University. The analysis, conducted by academics at the Wales Governance Centre, reveals the share of people experiencing severe mental health issues increased from 11.7% during the period immediately before the pandemic to 28.1% by April 2020. Covering the pre-COVID-19 pandemic period (2009–2019) and during COVID-19 pandemic (April 2020 to March 2021) the team aimed to quantify the impact of the pandemic, lockdowns and social restrictions on mental health in Wales.

The report found:

❖ The share of people in Wales reporting severe mental health problems climbed from 11.7% pre- pandemic to 28.1% by April 2020.

- ❖ Young adults aged 16–24 experienced the largest deterioration in their mental health as a result of COVID-19, with their average indicator worsening by 24% relative to the pre-pandemic period.
- ❖ On average, women exhibited worse levels of mental health after the onset of the pandemic compared to men. However, it is important to consider the potential under-reporting of mental health issues of men.
- ❖ By June 2020, Black, Asian, and Minority Ethnic individuals in Wales reported on average more than 4.1 problems associated with mental distress, while White British reported 2.7, a difference of 55% in relative terms.
- ❖ The mental health gap between those on the lowest and highest incomes widened significantly during the pandemic. Mental health scores for people on low incomes worsened by 39% by November 2020, compared to by 6.5% deterioration for the highest income earners.

The report follows the team's analyses of future budgetary pressures on the Welsh Government, published in April 2021. Among those was a report on the NHS and the Welsh Budget, which identified significant pressures and demand for mental health services in Wales over coming years.

While all parts of the Welsh population experienced ill mental health to some degree during the pandemic and accompanying lockdowns, the report highlights the disproportionate impacts on women, younger adults, low-income earners and those from Black, Asian and Minority Ethnic backgrounds. Researchers say the findings highlight a crucial public health challenge for Wales in years to come as mental health is a key determinant of educational success, future earnings, employment and physical health of an individual. To address these challenges, organisations can adopt a trauma-informed approach. Being trauma-informed means recognising the signs and symptoms of trauma and creating an environment that promotes healing and resilience. A trauma-informed organisation aims to create a safe and supportive culture that acknowledges the prevalence of trauma in society while empowering individuals to seek help when needed. It means understanding that trauma is a pervasive aspect of human experience and taking steps to ensure that services provided are sensitive to its impact.

TRAUMA AND ADVERSITY

Trauma and adversity are growing public health concerns that impact all. Using a trauma-informed approach in organisations, systems of care, schools, hospitals and businesses is critical to the persistence of a movement – one of universal precaution, which involves all of us. In this chapter, we delve into the complex and multifaceted world of trauma and adversity, seeking to deepen our understanding of their profound impact on individuals' lives. Through an exploration of key concepts and insights from psychological research, we aim to provide a comprehensive overview that will enhance your knowledge and awareness of these critical topics. As we embark on this exploration of trauma and adversity, we invite you to open your mind and engage with the complexities of these topics. By delving into the various dimensions of trauma and adversity, we can deepen our understanding, challenge preconceptions and lay the groundwork for implementing trauma-informed approaches in the chapters that follow. Together, we can strive to create a world where compassion, understanding and healing are at the forefront of our interactions with individuals who have experienced trauma and adversity.

How Do We Define Trauma and Adversity?

Trauma and adversity are complex concepts that encompass a wide range of experiences and emotions. Trauma can be defined as an emotional response to a deeply distressing or disturbing event, such as violence, abuse, accidents, natural disasters or loss of a loved one. It is important to recognise that trauma is not solely based on the event itself but also on how the individual perceives and reacts to it.

Adversity, on the other hand, refers to challenging circumstances or misfortunes that individuals face throughout their lives which may include poverty, discrimination, chronic illness or disability.

Understanding trauma and adversity involves acknowledging their pervasive impacts on various aspects of an individual's life – physical health, mental well-being, relationships and overall functioning. People who experience traumatic events may develop post-traumatic stress disorder (PTSD), depression, anxiety disorders or other psychological issues. These reactions can manifest in various ways such as flashbacks, nightmares, difficulty concentrating or forming new memories, feelings of guilt or shame and even suicidal thoughts. Similarly, adversity can challenge an individual's ability to cope with everyday demands and may lead to negative outcomes in terms of mental health and social development. For instance, children growing up in poverty are more likely to exhibit behavioural problems and struggle academically compared to their peers from higher-income families.

To address trauma and adversity effectively, it is crucial for healthcare providers, educators, and policymakers alike to adopt a holistic approach that considers the unique needs of each individual affected by these experiences. This entails developing evidence-based interventions that can foster resilience among those facing adverse situations while providing adequate support for individuals grappling with the aftermath of traumatic events. Early identification of trauma-related symptoms can pave the way for timely access to appropriate therapeutic services which ultimately help mitigate long-term negative consequences.

How Does Trauma and Adversity Impact Our Lives?

Trauma and adversity have a significant impact on society, affecting not only the individuals who directly experience them but also the communities in which they live. When people undergo traumatic experiences such as abuse, violence or loss, it can lead to a wide range of emotional, psychological and physical consequences. These effects can manifest in various ways: mental health disorders like depression, anxiety and post-traumatic stress disorder (PTSD), substance abuse issues, and even chronic physical conditions such as cardiovascular disease or obesity. The ripple effect of trauma extends beyond individual suffering to touch entire communities. For example, children exposed to adverse experiences are more likely to struggle academically and exhibit behavioural problems at school. This can disrupt classrooms and create challenges for educators tasked with balancing the needs of diverse learners. Moreover, these children may struggle to form healthy relationships with peers due to their own unresolved trauma-related emotions.

In addition to impacting educational settings, trauma-induced behaviours might contribute to broader societal issues such as crime rates and poverty levels. When individuals affected by trauma turn to drugs or alcohol as coping mechanisms or engage in risky behaviours that jeopardise their safety or stability, this can perpetuate cycles of disadvantage both for themselves and their families. Furthermore, research has shown that exposure to childhood adversity is linked with an increased likelihood of criminal behaviour in adulthood – suggesting that addressing the root causes of trauma could play a crucial role in reducing crime rates. Another way in which trauma affects society is through its financial burden on public resources. The healthcare system bears much of this cost as it provides treatment for those dealing with mental health disorders resulting from traumatic experiences. Additionally, social services agencies must work tirelessly to support families disrupted by addiction or other negative outcomes caused by unaddressed trauma.

Law enforcement agencies are also impacted when they confront the aftermath of untreated trauma manifesting as criminal activity or domestic violence incidents. The prevalence of trauma necessitates comprehensive solutions that address its roots while also tending to those who have already been affected. This includes implementing preventative measures such as early intervention programmes, improving access to mental health services for all members of society, and offering support systems that help individuals build resilience in the face of adversity. By taking a proactive approach to addressing trauma and its impacts on society, we can foster healthier communities marked by empathy, understanding and collective healing. Ultimately, the effects of trauma on society are widespread and multifaceted – touching upon education, crime rates, public health expenditures and more. However, recognising these connections presents an opportunity for positive change: by investing in resources that promote prevention and recovery from traumatic experiences at both individual and community levels, we can work towards a brighter future marked by greater well-being for everyone.

In the Home

Trauma and adversity play a significant role in the home environment, often leading to increased stress levels, strained relationships and negative behavioural patterns. When families are faced with challenging situations like the cost-of-living crisis, they may experience financial difficulties that can exacerbate existing problems or create new challenges within the household. The anxiety of not being able to afford basic necessities such as food, shelter and healthcare can lead to feelings of helplessness and depression among family members. Children exposed to such hardships at an early age may suffer from long-lasting emotional and psychological effects due to witnessing their parents' struggles. Furthermore, these difficult circumstances can intensify conflicts between spouses or partners, resulting in a tense atmosphere that affects everyone in the household. In some cases, trauma and adversity may even contribute to substance abuse or domestic violence issues as individuals attempt to cope with their overwhelming emotions.

In the short term, traumatic events can cause immediate disruptions to daily life, such as temporary displacement of people during natural disasters or loss of jobs due to economic downturns. These disruptions often lead to heightened stress levels among affected populations, resulting in increased rates of mental health issues like anxiety and depression. Additionally, trauma can exacerbate existing social inequalities by disproportionately affecting marginalised communities who may already be struggling with poverty, discrimination or other forms of disadvantage. In the long term, traumatic events and adversity can leave lasting scars on individuals and societies. One key example is the way that trauma from war or political violence can lead to cycles of conflict passed down through generations. Children who witness violence or are forced to participate in it may grow up with deep psychological wounds that affect their ability to form healthy relationships or contribute positively to society. This intergenerational transmission of trauma can perpetuate cycles of violence and instability in regions afflicted by conflict.

Overall, the impact of trauma and adversity on families experiencing economic hardships is multifaceted and deeply rooted. When someone experiences trauma or adverse events, it can lead to a range of emotional, psychological and behavioural reactions. The individual may develop post-traumatic stress disorder (PTSD), anxiety, depression or other mental health issues as a result of the traumatic event. These conditions can cause them to experience flashbacks, nightmares, mood swings, irritability, and difficulty concentrating or sleeping. In turn, these symptoms can affect their ability to function in daily life and maintain healthy relationships with friends and family. Friends and family members are often directly affected by the individual's trauma as well. They may struggle to understand what the person is going through or feel unsure about how to offer support. This uncertainty can lead to feelings of helplessness or frustration for both parties involved. Additionally, witnessing a loved one suffer from the effects of trauma can be emotionally challenging, in its own right.

Friends and family may also experience secondary traumatisation – meaning they begin to exhibit symptoms similar to those of the individual who experienced the initial trauma – as they empathise with their loved one's pain. Carers for individuals experiencing trauma face unique challenges as well. They must balance providing emotional support while also addressing practical needs such as medication management or assistance with daily activities. This responsibility can be overwhelming at times, leading carers to experience burnout or compassion fatigue – a state characterised by emotional exhaustion from caring for others in distressing situations. In some cases, carers may even develop vicarious traumatisation – a condition where they begin to internalise their clients' traumatic experiences as if they were their own. The ripple effect of trauma extends beyond just the individual experiencing it; it impacts everyone in their circle of support. As each person grapples with the consequences of adversity, communication within families may break down due to misunderstandings or misplaced blame. It is crucial for all members involved – individuals, friends, family, and carers – to seek appropriate support and resources to help navigate the challenges that arise from trauma.

In the Workplace

Trauma and adversity can significantly impact the workplace, affecting both staff and leadership. When employees experience traumatic events or face adversity in their personal lives, it may lead to a decrease in productivity, increased absenteeism and difficulties with concentration and decision-making. Additionally, employees who are struggling with trauma or adversity may display emotional instability or have difficulty maintaining healthy relationships with coworkers. This can create a tense working environment that negatively impacts morale and overall job satisfaction. Furthermore, leaders experiencing trauma and adversity may struggle to effectively manage their teams, communicate expectations clearly or make strategic decisions for the organisation's future success. The cost-of-living crisis serves as an example of how financial strain caused by trauma and adversity can put immense pressure on organisations. Staff members facing economic hardship due to rising living costs might be preoccupied with financial stressors and less able to focus on their work responsibilities fully. This decreased productivity could translate into reduced revenue for the organisation. Moreover, companies may need to invest additional resources in supporting employee mental health through counselling services or other assistance programmes to address the effects of trauma and adversity. The financial burden placed on these organisations could inhibit growth opportunities, limit budgetary flexibility and ultimately threaten long-term stability.

Aside from impacting individual workplaces directly, the widespread prevalence of trauma and adversity also places a significant burden on public services such as healthcare systems, social welfare programmes and educational institutions. As people struggle with the psychological ramifications of traumatic experiences or adverse situations like the cost-of-living crisis, they often require support from various public agencies to cope with these challenges effectively. For instance, individuals grappling with mental health issues resulting from trauma may seek treatment from publicly funded mental health clinics while those facing financial instability might rely on government-sponsored food assistance programmes. Unfortunately, this increased demand for public services often strains already limited resources and can contribute to longer wait times for care, decreased quality of service delivery or even programme cuts due to budget constraints. Consequently, the burden placed on public services by trauma and adversity not only affects those directly experiencing these challenges but also has broader implications for society as a whole. Inadequate support systems can perpetuate cycles of poverty, mental illness and other negative outcomes that ultimately undermine community resilience and limit opportunities for collective growth and prosperity within an organisation.

In the Community

The prolonged period of austerity in the United Kingdom has had a significant impact on communities and neighbourhoods, particularly in terms of trauma and adversity. One of the most notable impacts of this economic climate is the increased level of trauma and adversity faced by residents, particularly those living in vulnerable neighbourhoods. This heightened vulnerability often results from a combination of factors such as reduced social support networks, limited access to quality education and employment opportunities, and an overall decline in living conditions. As a result of these pressures, many individuals and families find themselves struggling to cope with day-to-day challenges, with some experiencing a breakdown within the family or relationships which can lead to an array of mental health issues such as stress, anxiety, depression or PTSD.

These psychological burdens have far-reaching implications for both the individual's well-being and the community at large. For instance, increased levels of crime and violence are often observed in areas where residents experience high degrees of economic hardship and social exclusion. Consequently, there is a higher demand for emergency services such as police response teams, ambulance services, and crisis intervention professionals who work tirelessly to address these complex situations. In addition to placing a strain on emergency response resources, this increase in crime and violence within vulnerable communities also puts additional pressure on social services. More specifically, organisations that provide housing assistance, counselling resources, food aid programmes or other basic needs may struggle to meet the demands of their clients due to limited funding and staff capacity. As a result, many people in need may not receive adequate support during times when they require it the most.

Furthermore, when neighbourhoods become victims of crime and violence, it has long-lasting effects on their reputation and sense of identity. The fear associated with being a target can erode trust among neighbours and discourage new investments or development projects that could contribute positively to local economies. In turn, this perpetuates cycles of poverty and disadvantage that undermine any efforts made towards achieving greater social cohesion or equality within society as a whole. The burden placed on public services, such as the police, ambulance and social services, also has ripple effects on other aspects of community life. For example, when these agencies are stretched thin due to high crime rates in vulnerable neighbourhoods, they may have less time and resources available to focus on preventative measures or proactive engagement strategies. This can result in a reactive approach to addressing issues within the community that often fails to address the root causes of crime and violence. Moreover, residents living in vulnerable neighbourhoods that experience higher levels of trauma and adversity may also face increased stigmatisation from those outside their communities. This stigma can manifest itself through negative stereotypes or assumptions made about individuals based solely on their residential location or demographic background. Such prejudices can further limit access to resources and opportunities for those living in these areas while exacerbating feelings of isolation and hopelessness amongst residents.

In the Global Context

The ongoing COVID-19 pandemic serves as an illustrative example of how trauma and adversity can impact a global context. The short-term effects include widespread job losses, business closures and economic recessions across multiple countries. Healthcare systems have also been overwhelmed, leading many individuals unable to access necessary medical care for unrelated conditions. Moreover, the pandemic has highlighted pre-existing disparities within societies; underprivileged groups have experienced higher death rates from COVID-19 due to living conditions, lack of access to healthcare resources or employment in high-risk essential worker roles. On a larger scale, the world has witnessed how national responses to the pandemic have exposed underlying tensions between nations. Geopolitical tensions have risen over trade disputes related to medical supplies and vaccines while debates surrounding border control measures continue to fuel anxieties about immigration policy and international relations more broadly. Consequently, these developments may contribute towards establishing new patterns in global politics that could last well beyond the end of the pandemic.

In terms of long-term consequences, the impact of COVID-19 on mental health is a significant concern. Prolonged periods of social isolation, financial stress and loss have left millions grappling with anxiety, depression and grief. The global rise in domestic violence during lockdowns highlights another dark aspect of the pandemic's effects on individuals and families. It remains to be seen how societies will address these widespread mental health issues post-pandemic. Additionally, the economic fallout from COVID-19 could lead to lasting changes in labour markets, social structures and international relations. For instance, increased automation and remote work may contribute to higher rates of unemployment or a widening wealth gap between those who can adapt to new technologies and those who cannot. In turn, this may trigger political unrest or social upheaval as people struggle to cope with these rapid societal shifts. The educational sector has also been profoundly affected by the pandemic, with students around the world experiencing disruptions in their learning due to school closures and remote education challenges. This could result in long-term negative consequences for children's academic achievement and future job prospects, particularly for those from disadvantaged backgrounds who lack access to resources like reliable internet connections or adequate support systems at home.

In conclusion, trauma and adversity have wide-ranging implications on both individual lives and broader societal structures. The ongoing COVID-19 pandemic has demonstrated how traumatic events can exacerbate existing inequalities while creating new tensions between nations and within communities. As we continue to navigate the complex ramifications of such large-scale crises, it is essential that efforts are made to mitigate their short-term impacts while addressing underlying factors that perpetuate cycles of trauma and adversity on a global scale. Ultimately, addressing these issues requires collaboration between governments, organisations and individuals to foster resilience and support for those affected by trauma and adversity. By understanding the interconnected nature of our world and working together to promote healing and growth, we can build a more equitable and compassionate global community capable of weathering future challenges.

What Is 'Re-traumatisation'?

Re-traumatisation is a psychological phenomenon that occurs when an individual who has experienced a traumatic event in the past is exposed to new situations or stimuli that trigger memories of the initial trauma. This can lead to a resurgence of symptoms associated with post-traumatic stress disorder (PTSD), such as flashbacks, nightmares, intrusive thoughts and heightened emotional arousal. Re-traumatisation can have significant consequences on an individual's mental health, relationships and overall quality of life. The process of re-traumatisation often begins with the activation of memory networks related to the original traumatic experience. These memory networks are composed of sensory information, emotions and cognitive appraisals that were encoded during the trauma. When a person encounters a situation or stimulus that shares similar characteristics with their past trauma, these memory networks may be activated and cause the individual to relive aspects of the traumatic event. This can result in both physiological responses, such as increased heart rate and hyperventilation, as well as psychological reactions like fear, anxiety and feelings of helplessness. There are several factors that contribute to an individual's vulnerability to re-traumatisation. One key factor is the severity of the original trauma; individuals who have experienced more severe forms of trauma are at greater risk for becoming re- traumatised. Additionally, those who have not had adequate opportunities to process their traumatic experiences through therapeutic interventions or supportive social environments may also be more susceptible to re-traumatisation. Finally, personality traits such as high levels of neuroticism and low levels of resilience can predispose individuals to experience further distress when confronted with reminders of their past traumas.

Preventing re-traumatisation requires addressing both internal and external sources of risk. On an individual level, engaging in evidence-based treatments for PTSD such as cognitive behavioural therapy (CBT) or eye movement desensitisation and reprocessing (EMDR) can help individuals develop healthier coping strategies for managing their traumatic memories. Furthermore, practicing self-care strategies like mindfulness meditation, exercise, and maintaining a strong social support network can help strengthen an individual's psychological resilience and reduce the likelihood of re-traumatisation. On a societal level, it is crucial to create environments that minimise the potential for triggering individuals who have experienced trauma. This may involve implementing trauma-informed care practices in settings such as hospitals, schools and prisons, which emphasise creating safe spaces and avoiding unintentional re- traumatisation through insensitive or harmful practices. Additionally, raising awareness about the prevalence of PTSD and promoting empathetic understanding of its effects can help reduce stigmatisation and encourage those affected by trauma to seek appropriate support. In cases where re- traumatisation does occur, it is important for individuals to recognise the signs of this phenomenon and seek appropriate professional help if necessary. Mental health professionals trained in working with trauma survivors can provide targeted interventions to address symptoms associated with re- traumatisation and promote healing from the original traumatic experience. Likewise, friends and family members can play a vital role in providing emotional support during these challenging times.

TRAUMA-INFORMED CARE & PRACTICE

Trauma-informed care (TIC) and trauma-informed practice (TIP) may sound like the same concept, however, while intertwined they are distinct in various way. In this chapter, we embark on a journey of discovery into the principles and practices of trauma-informed care and trauma-informed practice. By delving into the core concepts, approaches, and strategies, we aim to equip organisations, authorities, and person- facing professionals with the knowledge and tools necessary to create safe, supportive, and healing environments for individuals affected by trauma. As we delve into the realm of trauma-informed practice and trauma-informed care, we invite you to embrace a mindset of compassion, empathy and continuous learning. By incorporating trauma-informed principles and strategies into your professional practice, you have the power to make a profound difference in the lives of individuals impacted by trauma. Together, let us navigate this chapter, embracing the transformative potential of trauma-informed care, and working towards creating a more supportive and resilient society.

Trauma-informed Care

Trauma-informed care (TIC) is like reshaping the garden of support and healing. It goes beyond individual interactions and becomes an entire way of thinking, transforming the way we approach those in need. Imagine this as a process of shifting from asking, 'What is wrong with you?' to a more empathetic, 'What has happened to you?' This transition requires us to reorganise the way we work together, making our environment more collaborative and less hierarchical. TIC is built upon a foundation of understanding that everyone has a story, and it might include challenging experiences that have left lasting marks. Just as a reflective gardener learns about each plant's needs, TIC encourages professionals to reflect on their practice, adapting a strengths-based model that promotes safety and well-being.

Think of 'universal precaution' in medicine – it's like putting on gloves to protect against possible hazards. In the same way, TIC operates as a universal precaution for emotional well-being. Instead of gloves, professionals metaphorically 'glove up' by changing their approach – interactions, policies, procedures – to create a space that assumes everyone has faced trauma. It's a safeguarding measure to prevent inadvertently causing distress or re-traumatisation. This approach reshapes the entire garden of care. The hierarchy becomes more of a level field, where collaboration blooms. Professionals and caregivers listen more attentively, validate experiences and invite individuals to take an active role in their healing journey. Just as a well-kept garden yields vibrant flowers, TIC helps individuals flourish by reducing stress, building resilience and fostering healthier relationships. In a world where understanding and compassion are essential, trauma-informed care serves as the gardener's touch, cultivating hope and healing for all who seek solace and support.

Trauma-informed Practice

Imagine you have a friend who's been through some really tough experiences in their life, like accidents, abuse or other distressing events. These experiences can have a big impact on how they feel and behave. Trauma-informed practice is like a way of doing things that takes into account the fact that people might have gone through these difficult times. But it's not about directly treating the trauma itself. Instead, it focuses on making sure that when your friend needs help or support – like from doctors, teachers or counsellors – they don't face additional barriers because of what they've been through.

Trauma-informed practice operates with a distinct focus – it doesn't specifically target the treatment of trauma-related difficulties. Instead, it sets its sights on dismantling the obstacles that individuals impacted by trauma might encounter when seeking the care, support and treatment essential for a balanced and healthy life. This approach stands in contrast to trauma-specific services, which are specialised in providing explicit support or treatment to those profoundly affected by their traumatic experiences. This differentiation allows us to discern between trauma-informed services, such as those administered by health boards, which are geared towards addressing the repercussions of trauma through the utilisation of tailored therapies and other dedicated approaches. At its core, trauma-informed practice (TIP) embodies a comprehensive comprehension of how exposure to trauma influences various facets of an individual's development, encompassing neurological, biological, psychological and social dimensions.

This model draws upon insights from neuroscience, psychology, social science as well as theories related to attachment and trauma. Notably, it acknowledges the profound and intricate impact that trauma can have on an individual's perceptions of the world and their connections with others. This framework extends its applicability across all spheres of public service, including social care, physical health, housing, education and the criminal justice system. A fundamental assumption underlying trauma-informed organisations is that individuals have encountered traumatic events. These experiences may render it challenging for them to experience a sense of safety within the framework of services and to foster trusting relationships with those offering assistance. Consequently, trauma-informed practices involve meticulous structuring, organisation, and delivery of services, all orchestrated to cultivate an environment that prioritises safety and engenders trust. The overarching goal is to prevent any potential re-traumatisation, ensuring that individuals can engage with services in a way that promotes their well-being and healing.

Trauma-informed practice is about changing the way we approach everything across different fields, like healthcare, education and social services. It's not just a single method or therapy. It's a way of thinking that's based on understanding how trauma can affect a person's brain, body, emotions and relationships. This approach includes knowledge from areas like neuroscience (how the brain works), psychology (how emotions and thoughts work) and social science (how people interact with each other). On the other hand, trauma-informed care is more specific. It's like a special type of service that's designed to directly help people who have been deeply affected by their traumatic experiences. These services use specific therapies and methods to address the impact of trauma and help individuals heal from it. So, trauma-informed care is like a focused approach that's meant to provide targeted support to those who need it the most. In a nutshell, trauma-informed practice is like changing the way we do things in various areas to make sure people who have experienced trauma feel safe and supported. Trauma-informed care, however, is a more specialised approach that directly aims to help individuals who are dealing with the effects of trauma. Both are important, but they focus on different aspects of helping people who've been through tough times.

Trauma-informed practice is an essential aspect of any non-clinical organisation seeking to effectively support and empower individuals who have experienced trauma. By adopting key principles such as safety, trustworthiness, choice, collaboration, empowerment and culture sensitivity, organisations can create an environment that promotes healing and nurtures the well-being of those impacted by traumatic experiences. It is also important for non-clinical organisations to recognise that implementing trauma- informed practices transcends individual actions or isolated initiatives; rather, it requires a systemic transformation at all levels of the organisation. This involves revisiting organisational values, mission statements and strategic plans to ensure alignment with the principles of safety, trustworthiness, choice, collaboration, empowerment and cultural sensitivity. Moreover, it calls for embedding these principles into routine decision-making processes across various functions – from human resource management to financial planning – so that they become an integral part of organisational life.

Guiding Principles of TIP & TIC

Although there may be differences in terms of their application, it is widely acknowledged that these principles are relevant across the public sector and its range of services. It is also recognised that the development of trauma-informed practice requires systematic alignment with these principles, along with change at every level of an organisation. For this reason, the implementation of TIP is often described as an ongoing process of organisational change, requiring a profound paradigm shift in knowledge, perspective, attitudes and skills that continues to deepen and unfold over time. Thus, the literature increasingly refers to a 'continuum' of implementation, where becoming trauma-informed is a journey, not a destination.

Safety

The importance of physical and emotional safety within an organisation cannot be overstated. Physical safety involves thinking about security and the aesthetics of the building itself (appearance, lighting, accessibility, etc.) and the effect that those may have on individuals.

Emotional safety can be ensured by being attentive to signs of individual discomfort, recognising these signs in a trauma-informed way, checking in, debriefing and providing support to staff, and ensuring interactions with everyone are welcoming, respectful and engaging. By prioritising the well-being of clients and staff through thoughtful consideration of their environment and interactions, organisations can foster a sense of security that ultimately leads to better outcomes for all involved. By incorporating trauma-informed practices and being attentive to individual needs, we can work towards creating spaces where everyone feels safe, respected and supported. This holistic approach to safety not only benefits individuals but also contributes to the overall success and effectiveness of an organisation, making it a vital component in any workplace or service setting.

Trustworthiness

Trustworthiness refers to the ability of an organisation or practitioner to be reliable, dependable and honest in their interactions with clients, colleagues and other stakeholders. This includes maintaining confidentiality, respecting boundaries and being transparent about the intentions behind actions and decisions. This involves providing clear information about what will be done, by whom, when why and under what circumstances (including role clarity, rules/ job descriptions, etc.). It also means maintaining respectful and professional boundaries, prioritising privacy and confidentiality, and ensuring interactions and rules are consistent with an emphasis placed on follow-through. Transparency plays a significant role in establishing trustworthiness within an organisation. By ensuring that all policies, procedures, and decision-making processes are clear and accessible to everyone involved, organisations can create a sense of openness and accountability. This helps to build trust among staff members as well as between the organisation and its clients or service users. When people feel confident that they understand how things work and why certain decisions are made, they are more likely to engage meaningfully with the services provided.

Choice

Trauma-informed organisations prioritise
the principle of choice to ensure that clients
and staff feel empowered, respected, and valued
in their decision-making processes. The concept
of choice is closely related to the idea of
autonomy, as it allows individuals to have
control over their own lives and experiences.
By providing meaningful choices for clients and
staff within an organisation, those in positions of
authority demonstrate a commitment to
fostering a safe and inclusive environment.
One aspect of this key principle involves actively
seeking input from clients and staff on decisions
that directly affect them. This can be achieved
through regular meetings, surveys, or suggestion
boxes where opinions and ideas can be shared
openly without fear of judgement or retribution.
Offering opportunities for feedback not only
establishes trust but also ensures diverse
perspectives are considered when implementing
changes within the organisation. Another
important element of choice within a trauma-
informed organisation is flexibility. Recognising
that no two individuals will have the same
needs or preferences means being open to
adapting services, policies, and procedures
accordingly.

Collaboration

This principle acknowledges that each person within the organisation, be it staff or clients, has unique experiences and perspectives that can contribute significantly to the betterment of services provided. In order to effectively implement collaboration within an organisation, it is essential to create open channels for communication and actively encourage input from all members. Another important aspect of collaboration involves flattening organisational hierarchies in order to empower all individuals within the system. Decision-making processes should include input from both staff members and clients alike so that everyone feels heard and valued. This involves the creation of an environment of doing with rather than doing to or for, giving all individuals a significant role in planning and evaluating their care or service, conveying the message that individuals are the experts in their own lives or roles. Eliciting feedback from all stakeholders is another critical component of successful collaboration within a trauma-informed organisation.

Regular evaluations should be conducted at every level – from individual care plans to overarching policies – in order to ensure that any necessary changes are made based on the collective wisdom gathered from those involved. This process not only leads to more effective service provision but also demonstrates a genuine commitment to continual improvement. This not only leads to better outcomes for clients but also fosters a culture of mutual respect and understanding amongst all members of the organisation, ultimately contributing to a more compassionate and effective system overall.

Empowerment

Empowerment pertains to recognising and building on individual strengths, skills, communicating realistic sense of hope for the future. Empowerment is different than cheerleading. Instead of giving someone a direct compliment or encouragement, empowerment is more about eliciting from the individual – asking them to come up with capacities. Empowerment also involves providing opportunities for personal growth and professional development. When people feel they have access to resources, support and opportunities to learn new skills or enhance existing ones, they are more likely to take charge of their own well-being and contribute positively to the organisation. This includes offering ongoing training opportunities for staff members as well as clients so that they can develop relevant knowledge and skills for success. In order to foster empowerment within a trauma-informed framework, it is crucial that organisations establish a culture of collaboration and inclusivity. This entails encouraging teamwork among employees or volunteers while actively seeking input from diverse perspectives. By doing so, not only will individuals within the system feel heard and valued but unique insights may emerge which could lead to innovative problem-solving approaches. Promoting self-advocacy is another critical component of empowerment in trauma-informed practice. Encouraging individuals to voice their needs, preferences and goals allows them to take ownership over their life circumstances or treatment plans. Additionally, this fosters a sense of autonomy in making informed decisions about one's own well-being. Lastly, recognising resilience plays a significant role in empowering individuals who have experienced trauma. Acknowledging the innate strength, it takes to survive traumatic events can provide hope for healing and recovery while validating their experiences. By focusing on building resilience rather than dwelling solely on past traumas or challenges faced by clients or staff members alike helps create an environment conducive to growth and empowerment.

Culture

This principle recognises that understanding a person's background, including their cultural upbringing, historical context and personal experiences, can significantly affect how trauma manifests in their lives. By considering these factors when addressing trauma-related issues, organisations can create more effective policies, protocols and processes tailored to meet the unique needs of each employee or client. It is essential for organisations to actively move past cultural stereotypes and biases based on race, gender, ethnicity, sexual orientation, age, religion, etc. These biases can be harmful to employees and clients alike as they might perpetuate discrimination and marginalisation. Instead of relying on such assumptions about individuals' backgrounds or identities, organisations should strive to learn about people's lived experiences by engaging in open conversations with them.

Moreover, incorporating policies that are responsive to the racial, ethnic and cultural needs of employees and clients demonstrates an organisation's commitment to inclusivity. Recognising and addressing historical traumas stemming from racism or discrimination fosters a sense of healing among those affected. For instance, acknowledging the intergenerational trauma of colonialism on Black, Asian and Minority Ethnic populations, and the intergenerational impacts of discrimination towards the LGBTQIA+ community, may help provide appropriate support services for these communities. Creating an inclusive workplace means not tolerating racism or discrimination in any form. Organisations must actively work to counter both hidden (implicit) and overt (explicit) biases through various methods such as diversity training programmes for staff members. Additionally, fostering a supportive environment where employees feel comfortable reporting instances of prejudice helps ensure everyone feels valued within the organisation. Another crucial aspect is recognising intersectionality – the idea that different aspects of a person's identity often intersect in ways that exacerbate their experience with trauma or discrimination. For example, a Black transgender woman may face additional challenges compared to someone who doesn't share these intersecting aspects of identity or experience marginalisation due to systemic oppression. Understanding these complex intersections can help organisations better support employees and clients from diverse backgrounds.

The Four Rs

Another guiding principle to keep in mind is the Four Rs of trauma-informed practice which are **Realise, Respond, Resist Re-traumatisation** and **Restore.** This principal aspect of trauma-informed practice is essential for any non-clinical organisation that aims to support and empower individuals who have experienced traumatic events. These practices enable organisations to demonstrate empathy, understanding, and commitment towards helping people heal from the effects of trauma.

❖ **Realising** the signs and symptoms of trauma in individuals is a crucial first step in adopting a trauma-informed approach. By educating staff members about common indicators such as anxiety, depression, substance abuse or difficulty forming relationships, organisations can better identify those who may be struggling with past traumas. This awareness allows staff members to interact more compassionately with these individuals and create a supportive environment where they feel safe and understood.

❖ **Responding** appropriately to individuals experiencing trauma-related distress involves providing validation, reassurance, and practical assistance when needed. Staff members should be trained in active listening skills, empathic communication techniques and ways to offer emotional support without becoming overwhelmed themselves. Encouraging open dialogue about an individual's experiences can help them process their emotions and reduce feelings of isolation or shame associated with the traumatic event.

❖ **Resisting re-traumatisation** is another important aspect of trauma-informed practice. Organisations must ensure their policies and procedures do not inadvertently trigger or exacerbate an individual's traumatic memories or reactions. For instance, it may involve offering alternative meeting spaces for someone who feels claustrophobic due to past confinement experiences or avoiding overly graphic content during presentations if it might cause distress for certain participants. Careful consideration must be taken when discussing sensitive topics so as not to cause additional harm.

❖ **Restoring** an individual's sense of safety and control is vital in supporting their healing journey. Providing resources such as self-help materials, referrals to appropriate therapeutic services, or peer support groups can empower survivors to take charge of their recovery process. It's also essential for organisations to create an inclusive culture that values diversity and fosters resilience among all members.

In summary, implementing the Four Rs of trauma-informed practice in non-clinical organisations requires a comprehensive approach that encompasses awareness, empathic response, prevention of re-traumatisation and support for recovery. By fostering a culture of understanding and compassion, these organisations can make a significant positive impact on the lives of individuals who have experienced trauma. This not only benefits the affected individuals but also contributes to creating healthier and more supportive communities overall.

The Impact of Trauma-informed Care and Practice

A review of the literature provides evidence that the implementation of trauma-informed practice and trauma-informed care in various settings has proven to be highly beneficial for individuals who have experienced traumatic events. These approaches promote a deeper understanding of the effects of trauma on a person's overall well-being and create environments that foster healing, resilience and empowerment. For trauma survivors, trauma-informed services can bring hope, empowerment and support that is not re-traumatising. Moreover, such services can help close the gap between the people who use services and the people who provide them. Through education and awareness-raising efforts, professionals in various fields such as healthcare, education and social services can become more sensitive to the needs of those affected by trauma. By incorporating principles of safety, trustworthiness, collaboration, choice and empowerment into their work, they are better equipped to provide support that is both effective and compassionate.

Furthermore, the adoption of trauma-informed practices encourages organisations to critically evaluate their policies and procedures to minimise potential triggers or re-traumatisation experiences for clients. In doing so, they contribute to creating safer spaces where survivors can feel understood and validated. Moreover, recognising the prevalence of trauma across different populations highlights the importance of universal precautions when working with others. This approach allows service providers to assume that any individual may have experienced some form of trauma without requiring them to disclose or discuss it openly. Such an attitude fosters respect for privacy while still ensuring appropriate support is offered. Ultimately, integrating trauma-informed practice and care within our systems paves the way for a more empathetic society that acknowledges the complex interplay between trauma and daily life. By fostering resilience in individuals and communities, we move closer to a world where all people have access to resources necessary for healing from past traumas and thriving in spite of adversity.

In the Home

Trauma-informed practice in an organisation can have a profound impact on the individuals who engage with it. This approach recognises that past experiences of trauma may affect how people interact with organisations and service providers, as well as their ability to access and benefit from services. As a result, individuals feel more comfortable sharing their story and trusting the professionals they interact with, which contributes to greater engagement in services and supports provided by the organisation. When an individual frequently engages with a trauma-informed organisation, they often experience positive outcomes that ripple into other aspects of their life. For example, improved mental health can lead to increased self-esteem, reduced anxiety or depression symptoms and better stress management skills. These improvements may enable some individuals to successfully re-enter educational or employment settings. With newfound stability and support from trauma-informed practices in place, people can build resilience and work towards achieving their personal goals for growth and development.

The benefits of engaging with trauma-informed organisations extend beyond the individual receiving services; families, friends and carers are also impacted positively by this approach. Family members often play an essential role in supporting loved ones who have experienced trauma; therefore, when service providers adopt trauma-informed practices, it eases the burden placed on those providing emotional support at home. Additionally, friends and carers benefit from witnessing the improvements in their loved one's well-being as they engage with these services. This can result in stronger relationships between all parties involved as everyone gains a deeper understanding of each other's needs and experiences related to past traumas.

Moreover, staff members working within trauma-informed organisations also experience positive impacts on their home lives due to this approach. Receptionists, social workers, teachers, housing officers – anyone interacting directly with clients – gains valuable insight into how to best serve those experiencing trauma-related issues. By incorporating these principles into daily interactions, staff members develop essential skills for empathetic communication and problem-solving. This not only benefits their professional lives but also translates into improved relationships with family and friends outside of work. Furthermore, working within a trauma-informed organisation often creates a more supportive and understanding workplace culture that prioritises employee well-being. When organisations acknowledge the potential impact of vicarious trauma on staff members, they are better equipped to provide resources and supports necessary to maintain mental health. This commitment to employee wellness can lead to higher job satisfaction, reduced burnout rates and absenteeism, while increasing overall happiness of both staff and clients alike.

In the Workplace

The importance of staff support in the context of a global pandemic has been particularly evident recently, with studies demonstrating that levels of stress and burnout are reduced among frontline workers when they feel well prepared for their role as a result of specialised training, or when they feel confident in their own knowledge and understanding of the situation. The importance of leaders that convey compassion and sensitivity has also been underlined, and evidence is growing that the nurturing of self-compassion among healthcare staff can enhance staff well-being. Recent studies have also suggested that the building of support mechanisms into daily work routines can provide space for staff to look out for each other and reflect on shared experiences, with reports that time spent on such exercises can result in significant improvements in staff well-being.

Services working with traumatised client groups are at risk of developing organisational and systemic trauma, developing parallel processes, and often seeing factors such as high staff turnover, sickness and difficult team dynamics as a result of being impacted upon by the demands of the work they are doing. Compassion Fatigue and Secondary/Vicarious Trauma are ongoing difficulties for staff working in this important field. Organisations and services can benefit enormously from developing a trauma-informed culture to ensure that they can prevent their services and staff from becoming trauma infused/soaked, overwhelmed by stress and compassion fatigue, and mirroring the processes of mistrust and disconnection. It is crucial for senior management teams, strategic leaders as well as front line and operational staff to have a trauma-informed, systemic understanding and consistent approach to their work to protect and safeguard their workforce as well as the vulnerable people they support. The benefits of adopting and developing a coherent organisational approach can ensure that the whole system can work together to support staff well-being, improve trust and connection in staff teams, and improve outcomes.

Additionally, an argument could also be made that an organisation that doesn't protect staff in this way could be subject to claims under employment legislation in the future. With regard to the benefits of trauma-informed practice for staff, evidence is emerging that people who work in human services have a high prevalence of ACE scores themselves. Healing thus becomes just as relevant to staff as it is to service users, making the provision of staff training, supervision and support of utmost importance. Indeed, organisations that do not support their staff to take care of themselves run the risk of exposing them to secondary traumatic stress, vicarious trauma and burnout, all of which will inhibit their ability to provide high-quality care.

In the Community

The impacts of adopting a trauma-informed approach within an organisation are profound, both on the local population and the organisation itself. By understanding the prevalence and effects of trauma, such organisations can foster resilience, promote healing, and ultimately contribute to building healthier communities. One of the most notable impacts of trauma-informed practice on the local population is increased awareness about the widespread nature of traumatic experiences. Many people are unaware that they have been affected by some form of trauma or how their past experiences might be influencing their present lives. As organisations implement trauma-informed practices, they help to destigmatise these issues and encourage open discussions around mental health.

This heightened awareness allows community members to better recognise signs of trauma in themselves and others, which can lead to earlier intervention and support. Another important impact is improved service delivery for those seeking assistance from non-clinical agencies. Organisations that adopt a trauma-informed approach are better equipped to identify and address the unique needs of individuals who have experienced traumatic events. These organisations often provide tailored services that take into account clients' specific histories, strengths and vulnerabilities while offering comprehensive support during challenging times. This individualised care results in more effective interventions and long-term outcomes for clients.

In addition to enhanced service provision, incorporating trauma-informed practices can also help reduce re-traumatisation among vulnerable populations. Traditional approaches may unintentionally exacerbate symptoms associated with (PTSD) or other related conditions due to a lack of understanding surrounding these complex issues.

By being mindful of potential triggers and creating environments that prioritise safety, trustworthiness, collaboration, empowerment, choice and cultural sensitivity; non-clinical organisations can minimise the risk of additional harm. On a broader scale, adopting trauma-informed practices within non-clinical organisations has the potential to positively impact public health outcomes across entire communities. By addressing the underlying causes of various social issues – such as substance abuse, homelessness, domestic violence or mental illness – these organisations can help reduce societal costs and break cycles of intergenerational trauma.

In turn, this contributes to building stronger, more resilient communities where all individuals have an opportunity to thrive. In summary, incorporating trauma-informed practices within non-clinical organisations offers numerous benefits for both service providers and the local population. These approaches foster greater understanding and compassion around the prevalence of traumatic experiences while promoting effective support systems that prioritise individualised care and minimise re-traumatisation risks. Ultimately, implementing trauma-informed strategies leads to healthier work environments for employees and assists in creating thriving communities characterised by resilience and healing.

In the Global Context

In the global context, utilising trauma-informed practices can lead to more effective interventions and support systems across various sectors, including healthcare, education, criminal justice and social services. The COVID-19 pandemic has served as a powerful example of how widespread traumatic events can affect societies around the world. The devastating health impacts of the virus itself have been compounded by economic downturns, job losses, isolation due to lockdown measures and increased stressors on families and relationships. These factors have led to a surge in mental health issues globally, highlighting the critical need for trauma-informed approaches in addressing these challenges. By incorporating trauma-informed principles into pandemic response efforts, governments and organisations can better cater their policies and programmes to promote recovery at both individual and community levels. For instance, healthcare providers could be trained in recognising signs of psychological distress related to COVID-19 experiences or pre-existing traumas. This would enable them to incorporate appropriate interventions when treating patients suffering from physical symptoms of the virus or providing mental health support during this difficult period.

In addition to direct healthcare services, other sectors can benefit from adopting trauma-informed practices during the pandemic. Educational institutions worldwide have seen disruptions due to remote learning requirements or closures altogether. Teachers equipped with knowledge about trauma's impact on a student's ability to learn may be able to adapt their teaching methods accordingly while offering additional resources or support when necessary. Moreover, law enforcement agencies should also recognise that incidents of domestic violence may increase during times of crisis like the COVID-19 pandemic. By understanding the complexities involved in such situations – including both perpetrator's and victim's potential histories of trauma – police officers can respond more empathetically and effectively to calls for assistance. Furthermore, social service organisations that provide essential support to vulnerable populations during the pandemic must also be prepared to address the increased demand for their services. By adopting trauma-informed practices in their work, these agencies can ensure that they are creating safe spaces where individuals feel comfortable seeking help and receiving the necessary resources to promote healing and recovery.

In summary, the global impact of COVID-19 has highlighted the importance of trauma-informed practice across various sectors. By understanding how traumatic experiences can affect a person's physical, emotional and mental well-being, professionals working in healthcare, education, law enforcement, and social services can better serve those impacted by both the direct and indirect consequences of unprecedented crisis. As we continue to navigate through these challenging times, it is vital that a global commitment towards implementing trauma-informed principles becomes an integral part of our collective response effort to foster resilience and promote healing within our communities. Furthermore, the allocation of resources to support trauma-informed approaches is essential in ensuring that individuals and communities can recover from the detrimental effects of the pandemic. By sharing knowledge and best practices across borders, we can strengthen our collective ability to address trauma at its core and build a more compassionate world. As we look towards the future, embracing trauma-informed practice on a global scale will not only help us heal from the current crisis but also better prepare us for any challenges that may lie ahead.

THE WELSH TRAUMA FRAMEWORK

The Welsh Trauma Framework is an innovative approach to addressing the complex and varied needs of individuals who have experienced trauma. This framework, developed in Wales, United Kingdom, has been designed to provide a comprehensive understanding of the impact of trauma on individuals, as well as offering guidance for professionals working with these individuals to ensure that they receive appropriate support and care. The framework consists of several key components: identification and assessment, interventions and treatments, workforce development, and monitoring and evaluation. One of the main aspects of the Welsh Trauma Framework is its focus on identification and assessment. This involves recognising signs and symptoms of trauma in individuals and providing them with appropriate assessments to determine their specific needs. This process also includes screening for potential traumatic experiences during routine health appointments or when accessing other services such as housing or education. By doing so, professionals can work together across various sectors to help identify those who may be impacted by trauma and ensure that they are directed towards suitable support services.

Another important component of the framework is its emphasis on interventions and treatments tailored specifically for those affected by trauma. These include evidence-based psychological therapies such as cognitive behavioural therapy (CBT) or eye movement desensitisation and reprocessing (EMDR), which have demonstrated effectiveness in addressing post-traumatic stress disorder (PTSD) symptoms among individuals who have experienced various forms of trauma. Additionally, the Welsh Trauma Framework acknowledges the importance of providing holistic support services that address not only mental health but also physical health, social well-being, housing stability, employment opportunities, etc., all critical factors that contribute to overall recovery from traumatic experiences.

Workforce development plays a crucial role within this framework too. Ensuring that professionals working with traumatised individuals are well-trained and possess relevant skills is essential in providing high-quality care. In order to achieve this goal, the Welsh government has invested significantly in developing training programmes focused on improving knowledge about trauma-informed practices amongst healthcare providers, educators, social workers, and other professionals working in sectors where they may come into contact with individuals affected by trauma. By equipping these professionals with the tools and knowledge necessary to recognise and address trauma-related needs, it is hoped that the overall quality of care provided to these individuals will improve. Finally, monitoring and evaluation are key aspects of the Welsh Trauma Framework. This involves tracking progress in implementing the framework's various components and gathering data on outcomes for individuals receiving support services. Regular evaluations ensure that interventions remain effective, allow for adjustments as needed and contribute to building a solid evidence base for best practices in trauma-informed care. Furthermore, this continuous process of assessment allows policymakers and service providers to identify potential gaps or areas requiring further development, ultimately leading to more comprehensive and efficient support systems for those affected by trauma.

In summary, the Welsh Trauma Framework offers a well-rounded approach towards addressing the complex needs of individuals who have experienced trauma. Its focus on early identification and assessment ensures timely access to appropriate support services. The emphasis on evidence-based treatments tailored specifically for traumatised individuals fosters positive recovery outcomes. Workforce development initiatives ensure that professionals are adequately equipped with relevant skills and knowledge required when working with this population, while monitoring and evaluation processes help maintain effectiveness and facilitate improvements in provision over time. Overall, the implementation of this framework represents a significant step forward in understanding and addressing trauma-related needs among the Welsh population, paving the way for improved mental health outcomes across society.

TRAUMA-INFORMED ORGANISATIONS

A trauma-informed organisation acknowledges the impact of trauma on clients and staff with a goal to change the culture of organisations to recognise and respond through leadership reviewing policies and procedures and more. Any organisation in multidisciplinary teamwork can be trauma-informed from police departments, child protection, prosecution, mental health, victim advocacy and medical. It also acknowledges the signs and symptoms of trauma in its clients, staff, and others involved with the organisation. A trauma-informed organisation is one that integrates knowledge about trauma into policies, procedures, and practices to create a culture of safety, empowerment, healing, education, and resilience.

Cost of Becoming Trauma-informed

The cost of becoming trauma-informed is a realistic consideration. But the cost should be weighed against the cost of the workplace concerns that employees' stress and trauma contributes to – not only the safety, absenteeism and productivity challenges mentioned above, but also the physical and mental toll on workers as human beings, which can also lead to problems like high turnover. One way to ensure that the cost-benefit analysis works in an organisation's favour is to avoid one-size-fits-all, or off-the-shelf programmes. Organisations need programmes tailored to their circumstances and business environment, and individuals need programmes that acknowledge their diversity – gender, ethnicity, race, age, language, etc. Organisational staff do not need to be trauma experts, but their employee assistance programme providers do. And any organisation should understand the principles and ethics of a trauma-informed care approach in the workplace. For some employees, that could mean the difference between quitting and showing up to work every day, ready to be engaged and productive. The costs of becoming a trauma-informed organisation can vary depending on the size and type of organisation, as well as the scope of changes needed to become fully trauma-informed. Some potential associated costs to consider include:

Training and education: Staff at all levels may need training in trauma-informed practices, which could involve hiring outside trainers or bringing in experts to provide in-house training.

Time and resources: Implementing trauma-informed practices may require significant time and resources, particularly if major changes are needed to organisational policies, procedures and culture.

Infrastructure upgrades: Organisations may need to make physical changes to their facilities to create environments that are more conducive to healing and recovery for those who have experienced trauma.

Hiring additional staff: Depending on the size and needs of the organisation, it may be necessary to hire additional staff members with expertise in trauma-informed care.

Ongoing evaluation and assessment: To ensure that trauma-informed practices are being implemented effectively, ongoing evaluation and assessment will likely be needed, which could also involve additional costs for data collection and analysis.

Overall, while there are likely to be some upfront costs associated with becoming a trauma-informed organisation, many believe that the long-term benefits – including improved outcomes for those who have experienced trauma – outweigh these initial investments.

Trauma-informed Organisational Models

The trauma-informed organisational model provides a framework for becoming a trauma-informed organisation. The model will allow an organisation to gain insight and direction needed during this organisational change process. **Note:** Many parts of your organisation and even yourself likely already reflect aspects of a trauma-informed approach. To help you identify what is already in place and how to move forward, the model consists of stages, key development areas and domains of consideration.

The trauma-informed organisational model consists of three stages and within these stages, there are ten key development areas that require a trauma-informed approach to bring about overall change. These development areas are the focus of this guide. Each key development area has one or more domains of consideration, which incorporate trauma-specific content and values of a trauma-informed approach.

The aim is to ensure that each development area is addressed comprehensively. It should be noted that creating and maintaining a trauma-informed organisational change process takes time, usually around three to five years depending on the organisation's size and structure. The rest of this document aims to help organisations consider each component (values and principles, level of trauma-informed approach, stage, key development area(s), and domain(s) of consideration) throughout the process in a timeframe that suits them best.

Although the manual is suitable for any professional position, we suggest that it be distributed to official leaders and designated individuals responsible for carrying out the implementation process because of its emphasis on organisational transformation.

We suggest the following steps for those utilising this:

1. Familiarise yourself with the Approach section, below.
2. Utilise Appendix A as an initial evaluation of your organisation/service's progress in each key development area.
   ❖ Observe what is currently functioning and consider which areas may be beneficial to focus on given current circumstances.

3. Explore the relevant sections of the manual for additional information, examples from the experiences, and tools and resources.

It is advisable for the individuals in charge of carrying out the implementation process to thoroughly read the entire narrative of this manual. This is essential in comprehending the overall concept of how to transform into a trauma-informed organisation/ service, which is vital for making informed decisions on who should be involved and where to start.

Approach

Evaluation is a key component of the trauma-informed approach. It allows an organisation or service to take a step back and reassess how trauma-informed they are. Evaluating how trauma-informed an organisation is, involves looking at the culture and climate, as well as its policies and procedures, through a trauma-informed lens. The evaluation process of this model's approach utilises an organisational assessment tool that seek feedback from staff members and occasionally clients, patients, students or consumers about their views on the five fundamental values and principles of being trauma-informed.

Additionally, we inquire about particular policies and procedures related to trauma and adversity, that are implemented in their respective work areas within the organisation. There are multiple trauma-informed organisational assessment tools to choose from, which will be discussed later in this guidance, within the key development areas. It is crucial to have a comprehensive assessment plan in place to measure the advancement and overall achievement of implementing trauma-informed change within an organisation. One key aspect of this plan involves conducting a baseline evaluation prior to initiating any trauma- informed training or implementation measures. This allows the organisation/service to utilise the results of the evaluation when making deliberate decisions about what areas to focus their energy and resources on first, based on reported strengths and areas for improvement. Along with identifying where to begin, the baseline evaluation can also serve as a reference point for tracking progress over time. Consistently monitoring progress through evaluating implementation steps (such as identifying what is working well and what needs adjustments) is essential for sustaining trauma-informed organisational change.

The five guiding values and principles proposed by Harris and Fallot (2001) serve as a universal framework applicable to any setting or institution. This framework can be implemented across all levels of the organisation, including worker-to-client, patient, student, consumer relationships, as well as worker-to- worker and leadership-to-worker interactions. Although organisations strive to implement all five values of trauma-informed practice, it may not be possible to use them in every interaction. The principles and values are closely linked and distinctive, allowing for adaptable implementation. For example, if regulations prevent offering choices, how can we ensure trustworthiness by informing the person about what they can expect or guarantee their emotional well-being during the process? A thorough understanding of each value and principle is essential to using them effectively.

Key Development Areas

Within the three stages of the trauma-informed organisational model are ten key development areas – specific aspects of organisational functioning that need to be addressed through a trauma-informed lens to best create overall trauma-informed organisational change. The key development areas are the heart of the model and this manual, as the narrative and tools will walk you through and help you plan for the details of each. The key development areas are listed and summarised below.

1. LEADING AND COMMUNICATING Involves having leadership/ administration buy-in, investment and consistent messaging around trauma-informed organisational change, and the presence of a committee/team leading the change process	2. HIRING AND ORIENTATION PRACTICES Involves ensuring hiring, new-hire orientation and other human resources practices are conducted in ways that are trauma-informed and trauma sensitive.
3. TRAINING THE WORKFORCE (CLINICAL AND NON-CLINICAL) Involves a realistic and sustainable plan for providing ongoing trauma-informed education and training to all levels of the workforce	4. ADDRESSING THE IMPACT OF THE WORK Involves increasing workforce awareness of how to prevent/ manage secondary traumatic stress, vicarious trauma and compassion fatigue, as well as implementing organisational/ system structures to help support workers and promote vicarious resilience/vicarious post-traumatic growth
5. ESTABLISHING A SAFE ENVIRONMENT Involves taking a deliberate look at the environment and atmosphere of the organisation/service to ensure that physical space/ aesthetics and culture are trauma- informed and trauma sensitive	6. SCREENING FOR TRAUMA Involves deciding whether or not screening for trauma and/ or adversity is appropriate in the organisation/ system, and if so, what tools and follow-up structures are in place to do so

7. Treating Trauma Involves having on-site trauma-specific treatment interventions or accessible referrals in place for individuals who are seeking treatment for their trauma	8. Collaborating with Others (Partners and Referrals) Involves building on or creating mechanisms with partner organisations/ systems to collaboratively ensure trauma-informed networks, communities, and systems
9. Reviewing Policies and Procedures Involves confirming that all policies, procedures and protocols are written and conducted in a way that is in line with a trauma-informed and trauma-sensitive approach.	10. Evaluating and Monitoring Progress – Involves having mechanisms in place to evaluate and monitor trauma-informed organisational change, as well as its impact on the organisation/service in relation to outcomes

Each key development area has one or more domains of consideration, which are domains of organisational change that SAMHSA infused with trauma-specific content and the values and principles of a trauma-informed approach.

Domains of Organisational Change

To adopt a trauma-informed approach, an organisation must make changes at multiple levels and align with the six key principles outlined earlier.

This guidance provides a framework for developing an organisational trauma-informed approach, which includes assessing the role of trauma and implementing an organisational assessment and development process. Public institutions, service sectors, health professionals and workforce are encouraged to examine their practices and implement a trauma-informed approach across all levels of their organisation. The ten domains of organisational change presented here are not meant as a checklist or prescriptive step-by-step process but have been identified in both the organisational change management literature and models for establishing trauma-informed care. These domains ensure organisational change structures within each of the key development areas – which may have multiple domains of consideration in each.

Governance and Leadership

The leadership and governance of the organisation, support and invest in implementing and sustaining trauma-informed practice. There is an identified point of responsibility within the organisation to lead and oversee this work. There is inclusion of the peer voice. Involves having leadership/administration buy-in, investment and consistent messaging around trauma-informed organisational change, and the presence of a committee/team leading the change process.

Policy

There are written policies and protocols establishing trauma-informed practice as an essential part of the organisational mission. Organisational procedures and cross-agency protocols reflect trauma-informed principles. Involves confirming that all policies, procedures, and protocols are written and conducted in a way that is in line with a trauma-informed and trauma-sensitive approach.

Environment

The organisation ensures that the physical environment promotes a sense of safety and collaboration. Staff and clients must experience the setting as safe, inviting and not a risk to their physical or psychological safety. This involves taking a deliberate look at the environment and atmosphere of the organisation to ensure that physical space and culture are trauma-informed and trauma- sensitive.

Engagement

People in recovery, trauma survivors, consumers and family members receiving services have significant involvement, voice and meaningful choice at all levels and in all areas of organisational functioning (e.g., programme design, implementation, service delivery, quality assurance, cultural competence, access to trauma-informed peer support, workforce development and evaluation).

Cross-sector Collaboration and Mutuality

Collaboration across sectors is built on a shared understanding of trauma and principles of a trauma- informed approach. While a trauma focus is not the stated mission of different service sectors, understanding how trauma impacts those served and integrating this knowledge across service sectors is critical. The organisation recognises that everyone has a role to play in a trauma-informed approach, no matter their level of seniority or power. This principle manifests itself through teamwork and appreciating each team member's role in accomplishing the overall mission of the organisation. Collaboration across sectors is built on a shared understanding of trauma and the principles of trauma-informed practice. Involves building on and/or creating mechanisms with partner organisations/systems
 to collaboratively ensure trauma-informed networks, communities and systems.

Screening

Where interventions are not being delivered in healthcare organisations, direct services are provided which are culturally appropriate and reflect trauma-informed practice principles. Involves deciding whether or not screening for trauma and adversity is appropriate in the organisation/ system, and if so, what tools and follow-up structures are in place to do so. When trauma-specific services are not available within the organisation, there is a trusted, effective referral system in place that facilitates connecting individuals with appropriate trauma treatment. Within clinical settings, practitioners use and are trained in interventions that are based on the best available empirical evidence and science, are culturally appropriate, and reflect the principles of trauma-informed practice.

Training and Development

Ensuring there is ongoing training in trauma and peer support. The organisation's human resource system incorporates trauma-informed principles in hiring, supervision and staff evaluation. Procedures are in place to support staff with trauma histories and those experiencing secondary traumatic stress or vicarious trauma, resulting from exposure to and working with individuals affected by trauma. Involves a realistic and sustainable plan for providing ongoing trauma-informed education and training to all levels of the workforce.

Monitoring and Quality Assurance

In conjunction with the already existing monitoring and tracking for quality and performance responsibilities. There is ongoing assessment, tracking and monitoring of trauma-informed principles and effective use of evidence-based trauma-specific practices and approaches. Involves increasing workforce awareness of how to prevent/ manage secondary traumatic stress, vicarious trauma, and compassion fatigue, as well as implementing organisational/system structures to help support workers and promote vicarious resilience/vicarious post-traumatic growth.

Finance

Financing structures are designed to support trauma-informed practice which includes resources for: staff training on trauma; key principles of trauma-informed practice; development of safe and appropriate facilities; establishment of peer support; provision of evidence-based screening, assessment, and supports; and development of trauma-informed cross-agency collaborations.

Evaluation

Measures and evaluation designs used to evaluate service or programme implementation and effectiveness reflect an understanding of trauma and appropriate trauma-oriented research. Involves having mechanisms in place to evaluate and monitor trauma-informed organisational change, as well as its impact on the organisation/service in relation to outcomes.

Stage of Implementation

While *Transforming Society* does not dive into the implementation of a trauma-informed organisational model, an accompanying implantation guide is currently in production which will not only complement *Transforming Society* but guide organisations through the process of becoming trauma-informed.

The three stages of the organisational model are: Preparation, Implementation and Continuation. The requirements, resources and considerations for implementing a trauma-sensitive change in an organisation vary depending on which stage the organisation is currently in. Nevertheless, successful implementation of organisational change necessitates accepting that it is a fluid, continual

process that should be regularly reevaluated.
As a result, the three stages are multidimensional
and adaptable. For example, today you may find
your organisation is in the Continuation stage in
one key development area, only to re-evaluate
down the road and find that something new needs
to be implemented – bringing that area to the
Implementation stage once more. Additionally, your
service may be in different stages, depending on
which key development area is being considered.

STAGE ONE – PREPARATION – Involves the
preparation and establishment of a foundation
for implementing trauma-informed changes
within an organisation or service.

STAGE TWO – IMPLEMENTATION – Organisation or
service implements action steps specific towards
implementing a trauma-informed approach to
organisational transformation.

STAGE THREE – CONTINUITY – Further integration
of trauma-informed practices into the organisation
or services fabric by establishing mechanisms to
consolidate gains, monitor progress and adjust
implementation as needed.

*It is important to note here that true organisational
change can take a minimum of three to five years,
depending on the size and structure of the organisation.*

TAKING THE NEXT STEP

This comprehensive introduction has provided organisations, authorities and individuals in person-facing roles with an advanced introduction to trauma and adversity, trauma-informed practice and the Welsh Trauma Framework. By exploring the benefits and importance of becoming a trauma-informed organisation or service and delving into the key development areas and domains of organisational change, readers have gained valuable insights into implementing trauma-informed approaches.

We understand that transitioning to a trauma-informed organisation or service is a significant undertaking, and to support you further, we have developed a three-stage Implementation Guide. This accompanying resource offers detailed guidance, step-by-step instructions and practical tools to assist you throughout the implementation process. It is designed to enhance your understanding and provide you with the resources necessary to effectively embed trauma-informed practices within your organisation.

By embracing trauma-informed approaches, organisations and individuals in person-facing roles have the opportunity to make a positive and lasting impact on the lives of those they serve. Recognising the diverse impacts of trauma and adversity and integrating the principles and values of trauma-informed practice, you can create an environment that fosters healing, resilience and well-being.

We hope this comprehensive guide, together with the accompanying Implementation Guide, will serve as valuable resources on your journey towards becoming a trauma-informed organisation or service. By implementing trauma-informed practices, you have the power to transform the experiences of individuals affected by trauma and adversity, and create a culture of understanding, support and growth. Thank you for your commitment to making a difference in the lives of others through trauma-informed approaches. Together, we can create a more compassionate and resilient society.

ADDITIONAL RESOURCES

Transforming Society: A Comprehensive Guide to Implementing a Trauma-Informed Organisational Model

Traumatic Stress Wales Specification

Welsh Trauma Framework

Welsh Trauma Consultation Report Scottish Government toolkit

Plymouth Trauma-informed Network – Plymouth City Council Health & Well-being board

Books to Discover

The Body Keeps the Score (van der Kolk)

The Deepest Well (Burke Harris)

Trauma and Recovery (Herman)

Trauma Stewardship (Lipsky & Burk)

Using Trauma Theory to Design Service Systems (Harris & Fallot)

Current Reports

❖ What Works to Prevent Adverse Childhood Experiences (ACEs) at the Community Level? An Evidence Review and Mapping Exercise

❖ Trauma and ACEs Informed Higher Education in Wales Vision Paper

❖ Risk of Post-traumatic Stress Disorder following Traumatic Events in a Community Sample. Epidemiology and Psychiatric Sciences

❖ Identifying Women's Pathways to Offending and the Primary Prevention and Early Intervention Opportunities for Women at Risk of Offending in Wales

❖ What Works in the Prevention and Early Intervention of ACEs at the Community Level? Identifying and Supporting Projects across Wales

❖ 'Trauma-informed': Identifying Key Language and Terminology through a Review of the Literature

❖ Discrimination and Adverse Childhood Experiences (ACEs) in the Lives of Child Refugees of the 1930s: Learning for the Present and the Future

❖ An exploration of the trauma-informed terminology and approaches being used by significant projects, programmes, and interventions in Wales

- ❖ Independent evaluation of online training and recommendations for further training and embedding trauma-sensitive approaches into the workplace
- ❖ Exploring the perspectives of providers of education and educational support services on their ability to meet the needs of sanctuary seeking primary school children in South Wales
- ❖ Adverse Childhood Experiences in child refugee and asylum-seeking populations
- ❖ An evaluation of Adverse Childhood Experiences (ACE)-informed School Approach in three secondary schools in Wales

REFERENCES

Alive and Well Communities Educational Leader's Workgroup. (n.d.). The Missouri Model for Trauma- Informed Schools. Alive and Well Communities.

Bailey, S., & West, M. (2020). Covid-19: why compassionate leadership matters in a crisis. Retrieved from www.kingsfund.org.uk/blog/2020/03/covid-19-crisis-compassionate-leadership.

Bloom, S. (2013). Creating Sanctuary: Toward the Evolution of Sane Societies. New York: Routledge.

Brooks, S., Rubin, G., & Greenberg, N. (2019). Traumatic stress within disaster exposed occupations: overview of the literature and suggestions for the management of traumatic stress in the workplace. British medical bulletin.

Chung, S., Domino, M., & Morrissey, J. (2009). Changes in Treatment Content of Services During Trauma- Informed Integrated Services for Women with Co-occurring Disorders. Community Mental Health Journal, 45(5), 375–384.

Cocozza, J., Jackson, E., Hennigan, K., Morrissey, J., Reed, B., Fallot, R., & Banks, S. (2005). Outcomes for women with co-occurring disorders and trauma: program-level effects. Journal of Substance Abuse Treatment, 28(2), 109–119.

Cole, C., Waterman, S., Stott, J., Saunders, R., Buckman, J., Pilling, S., & Wheatley, J. (2020). Adapting IAPT services to support frontline NHS staff during the Covid-19 pandemic: the Homerton Covid Psychological Support (HCPS) pathway. the Cognitive Behaviour Therapist, 13.

Cole, S., Eisner, A., Gregory, M., & Ristuccia, J. (2013). Helping Traumatised Children Learn 2: Creating and Advocating for Trauma-sensitive Schools. Boston, MA: Massachusetts Advocates for Children.

Concetta, P. (2018). Survivor's voices, personal communication, in Sweeney, A & Taggart, D. (2018). (Mis)understanding trauma-informed approaches in mental health. Journal of Mental Health, 27(5), 383- 87.

Dillon, J., Johnstone, L., & Longden, E. (2012). Trauma, dissociation, attachment & neuroscience: a new paradigm for understanding severe mental distress. Journal of Clinical Psychology, Counselling and Psychotherapy, 12, 145–155.

Domino, M E, Morrissey, J P, Chung, S, Huntington, N, Larson, M J & Russell, L A, (2005). Service use and costs for women with co-occurring mental and substance use disorders and a history of violence', Psychiatric Services, 2005, 56, pp 1223–32

Domino, M., Morrissey, J., Chung, S., & Nadlicki, T. (2006). Changes in service use during a trauma-informed intervention. Women and Health, 14(5), 105–22.

Elliot, D., Bjelajac, P., Fallot, R., Markoff, L., & Reed, B. (2005). Trauma-informed or trauma-denied: Principles and implementation of trauma-informed services. Journal of Community Psychology, 33(4), 461–477.

Ellis, W., Dietz W. (2017). A New Framework for Addressing Adverse Childhood and Community Experiences: The Building Community Resilience (BCR) Model. Academic Paediatrics. 17, 86–99

Esaki, N., & Larkin, H. (2013). Prevalence of adverse childhood experiences (ACEs) among child service providers. Families in Society, 94(1), 31–37.

Fallot, R., & Harris, M. (2006). Trauma-Informed Services: A Self-Assessment and Planning Protocol. Washington, D.C: Community Connections.

Fallot, R., & Harris, M. (2009). Creating Cultures of Trauma-Informed Care (CCTIC): a Self-Assessment and Planning Protocol. Washington, D.C: Community Connections.

Farragher, B., & Yanosy, S. (2005). Creating a trauma-sensitive culture in residential treatment. Therapeutic Communities, 26(1), 93–109.

Felitti, V., Anda, R. F., Nordenberg, D., Williamson, D., Spitz, A., Edwards, V., & Marks, J. (1998). Relationships of childhood abuse and household dysfunction to many of the leading causes of death in adults: The Adverse Childhood Experiences (ACE) Study. American Journal of Preventative Medicine, 14, 245–258.

Greenwald, R., Siradas, L., Schmitt, T., Reslan, S., Fierle, J., & Sande, B. (2012). Implementing trauma-informed treatment for youth in a residential facility: first-year outcomes. Residential Treatment for Children and Youth, 29(2),

Guarino, K., Soares, P., Konnath, K., Clervil, R., & Bassuk, E. (2009). Trauma-informed Organizational Toolkit.

Harper, K., Stalker, C., & Gadbois, S. (2008). Adults traumatized by child abuse: What survivors need from community-based mental health professionals. Journal of Mental Health, 17, 361–374.

Harris, M., & Fallot, R. (2001). Using Trauma Theory to design Service Systems. Sab Fransisco, CA: Jossey- Bass.

Huang, L., Pau, T., Flatow, R., DeVoursney, D., Afayee, S., & Nugent, A. (2012). Trauma-informed care Models compendium.

Kucharska, J. (2018). Cumulative trauma, gender discrimination and mental health: Journal of Mental Health, 27(5), 416–423. doi:10.1080/09638237.2017.14 17548

Lai, J., Ma, S., Wang, Y., Cai, Z., Hu, J., Wei, N. Tan, H. (2020). Factors associated with mental health outcomes among health care workers exposed to coronavirus disease. JAMA, 3(3).

Marryat, L., & Frank, J. (2019). Factors associated with adverse childhood experiences in Scottish children: a prospective cohort study. BMJ Paediatrics Open, 3(1). doi:10.1136/bmjpo-2018–000340

Maunder, R., Lancee, W., Balderson, K., Bennett, J., Borgundvaag, B., Evans, S.,… Hall, L. (2006).

Long- term psychological and occupational effects of providing hospital healthcare during SARS outbreak. Emerging Infectious Diseases, 12(12).

Mauritz, M., Goossens, P., Draijer, N., & van Achterberg, T. (2015). Prevalence of interpersonal trauma exposure and trauma-related disorders in severe mental illness. European Journal of Psychotraumatology, 4(1).

Menschner, C., & Maul, A. (2016a). Key ingredients for successful trauma-informed care implementation. Trenton: Centre for Health Care Strategies, Incorporated.

Menschner, C., & Maul, A. (2016b). Strategies for encouraging staff wellness in trauma-informed organizations. http://hmprg.org/wpcontent/themes/ HMPRG/backup/ACEs/Toolkit/ ATC- StaffWellness121316_FINAL.pdf

Messina, N., Calhoun, S., & Braithwaite, J. (2014). 2014. Trauma-informed treatment decreases posttraumatic stress disorder among women offenders, 15(1), 6–23.

Najavits, L. (2007). Seeking Safety: An evidence-based model for substance abuse and trauma/PTSD. In K. Witkiewitz, & G. Marlatt, Practical Resources for the mental health professional. Therapist's guide to evidence-based relapse prevention. Elsevier Academic Press.

National Child Traumatic Stress Network (NCTSN). (2011). Secondary traumatic stress: A fact sheet for child-serving professionals. Los Angeles, CA and Durham, NC. Retrieved from

NHS Education for Scotland (NES). (2016). National Trauma Training Programme. Retrieved from https://www.transformingpsychologicaltrauma.scot/.

Paterson, B. (2014). Mainstreaming Trauma, presented at the Psychological Trauma-Informed Care Conference, Stirling University.

Penney, D., & Cave, C. (2013). Becoming a Trauma-informed Peer-Run Organisation: A Self-Reflection Tool. Adapted for Mental Health Empowerment Project, Inc. from Creating Accessible, Culturally Relevant, Domestic Violence- and trauma-informed Agencies. ASRI and National Centre on Domestic Violence, Trauma and Mental Health.

Purtle J. (2018) Systematic Review of Evaluations of Trauma-Informed Organizational Interventions that include Staff Trainings. Trauma Violence Abuse. 2020 Oct;21(4):725–740. doi: 10.1177/1524838018791304.

Read, J. (2010). Can poverty drive you mad? 'Schizophrenia', socio-economic status, and the case for primary prevention. New Zealand Journal of Psychology, 39(2), 7–19.

Schachter, C., Stalker, C., Teram, E., Lasiuk, G., & Danilkewich, A. (2008). Handbook on Sensitive Practice for Healthcare Practitioner: Lessons from Adult Survivors of Childhood Sexual Abuse. Ottawa: Public Health Agency of Canada.

Shanafelt, T., Ripp, J., & Trockel, M. (2020). Understanding and Addressing Sources of Anxiety Among Health Care Professionals During the COVID-19 Pandemic. JAMA, 323.

Substance Abuse and Mental Health Services Administration (SAMHSA). (2014). SAMHSA's Concept of Trauma and Guidance for a Trauma-Informed Approach. Rockville, MD: Substance Abuse and Mental Health Services Administration.

The Scottish Government. (2017). Justice in Scotland: Vision and Priorities. Edinburgh: The Scottish Government.

The Scottish Government (2019). The Scottish Health Survey. A National Statistics Publication for Scotland. www.gov.scot

Treisman, K. (2018). Becoming a more culturally, adversity, and trauma-informed, infused, and

responsive organization. Winston Chirchill Memorial
Trust. Retrieved from https://www.wcmt.org.uk/sites/
default/files/reportdocuments/Treisman%20K%
202018%20Final.pdf

Weissbecker, I., & Clark, C. (2007). The impact
of violence and abuse on women's physical
health: can trauma-informed treatment make
a difference? Journal of Community Psychology,
35(7), 909–23.

Xie, Z., Jiuping, X., & Zhibin, W. (2017). Mental
health problems among survivors in hard-hit areas
of the 5.12 Wenchuan and 4.20 Lushan earthquakes.
Journal of Mental Health, 26(1), 43–49. doi:10.1080/0
9638237.2016.1276525

Thank you for taking the time to purchase this comprehensive introduction to understanding trauma adversity and the concept of being trauma informed. An Implementation Guide to becoming a trauma-informed organisation will be available soon should you wish to take the next step on this journey.

Milton Keynes UK
Ingram Content Group UK Ltd.
UKHW021842160224
437755UK00007B/44

9 781803 816777